CANADIAN RESOURCES

WATER

BY THE NUMBERS

Jason McClure

Weigl

Published by Weigl Educational Publishers Limited
6325 – 10 Street SE
Calgary, Alberta, Canada
T2H 2Z9

Website: www.weigl.ca

Library and Archives Canada Cataloguing in Publication

ISBN 978-1-77071-271-3 (hardcover)

ISBN 978-1-77071-272-0 (softcover)

ISBN 978-1-77071-273-7 (multi-user eBook)

Printed in the United States of America in
North Mankato, Minnesota

1 2 3 4 5 6 7 8 9 0   17 16 15 14 13

WEP130613

072013

Weigl acknowledges Getty Images as the primary supplier for this title.

Every reasonable effort has been made to trace ownership and to obtain permission to reprint copyright material. The publishers would be pleased to have any errors or omissions brought to their attention so that they may be corrected in subsequent printings.

We acknowledge the financial support of the Government of Canada through the Canada Book Fund for our publishing activities.

Project Coordinator
Megan Cuthbert

Art Director
Terry Paulhus

CANADIAN RESOURCES
WATER
BY THE NUMBERS

CONTENTS

Earth contains about 1.4 billion cubic kilometres of water.

Water Resources

"I believe that water will be during this century more important than oil."
Dr. Boutros Boutros Ghali, former United Nations Secretary General

Water is one of the most important resources on Earth. Water covers 70 percent of Earth's surface. Most of this water is found in the world's oceans. Ocean water is salt water, which is salty and undrinkable.

People need fresh water to survive. Only about 2.5 percent of the water on Earth is fresh water and only 0.007 percent of the water can be used by people. This is because about 99 percent of all fresh water is deep underground or trapped in ice, such as glaciers. The fresh water supply that is trapped deep underground is called **non-renewable** water.

The World's Water Supply

The world's water supply is divided into fresh water and salt water. Most of the world's water is salt water found in oceans and seas.

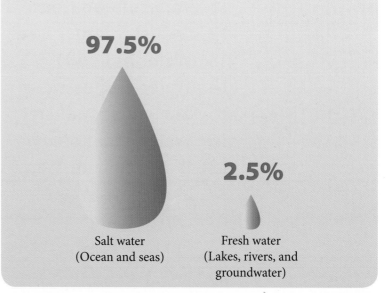

97.5%

Salt water
(Ocean and seas)

2.5%

Fresh water
(Lakes, rivers, and groundwater)

Usable Water

Renewable fresh water is water that falls as rain or snow. This is the water that keeps rivers filled. People rely on renewable fresh water for drinking and other uses. However, there are nearly 7 billion people in the world. Some scientists think the population will grow to 9 billion by 2050. All of these people need water, but the amount of fresh water is not changing. As the world's population continues to grow, so will the value of water.

The Great Lakes contain about 21 percent of the world's surface fresh water supply.

Amount of Renewable Fresh Water

The supply of renewable fresh water is spread across the world, but it is not spread evenly. This chart shows the six countries with the largest amounts of renewable fresh water. The amount of water is measured in cubic kilometres (km^3). One cubic kilometre of water is equal to the water in 400,000 Olympic-size pools.

Brazil
8,233 km^3

Russia
4,498 km^3

United States
3,069 km^3

Canada
3,300 km^3

China
2,830 km^3

Indonesia
2,838 km^3

Canada's Water Supply

Canada has about nine percent of the world's renewable fresh water. Counting both renewable and non-renewable water, Canada has about 20 percent of the world's fresh water. Each year, Canada's water supply is renewed by **precipitation**. Precipitation is not spread equally across the country. Many areas in Saskatchewan and Alberta do not get enough water for their needs. Other parts of the country, such as British Columbia and Nova Scotia, get plenty of rain and snow.

Another important source of water is groundwater. Groundwater is water that flows below the ground. This water can be accessed by digging wells. About 25 percent of Canadians get their water from groundwater sources.

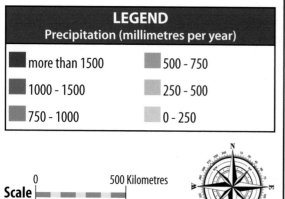

LEGEND	
Precipitation (millimetres per year)	
■ more than 1500	■ 500 – 750
■ 1000 – 1500	■ 250 – 500
■ 750 – 1000	■ 0 – 250

Scale

| 0 | 500 Kilometres |
| 0 | 310.7 Miles |

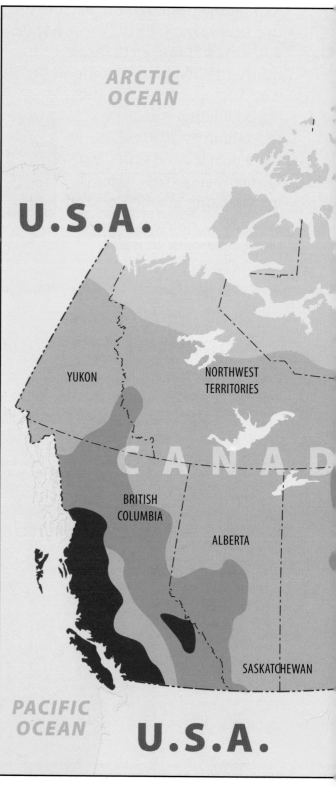

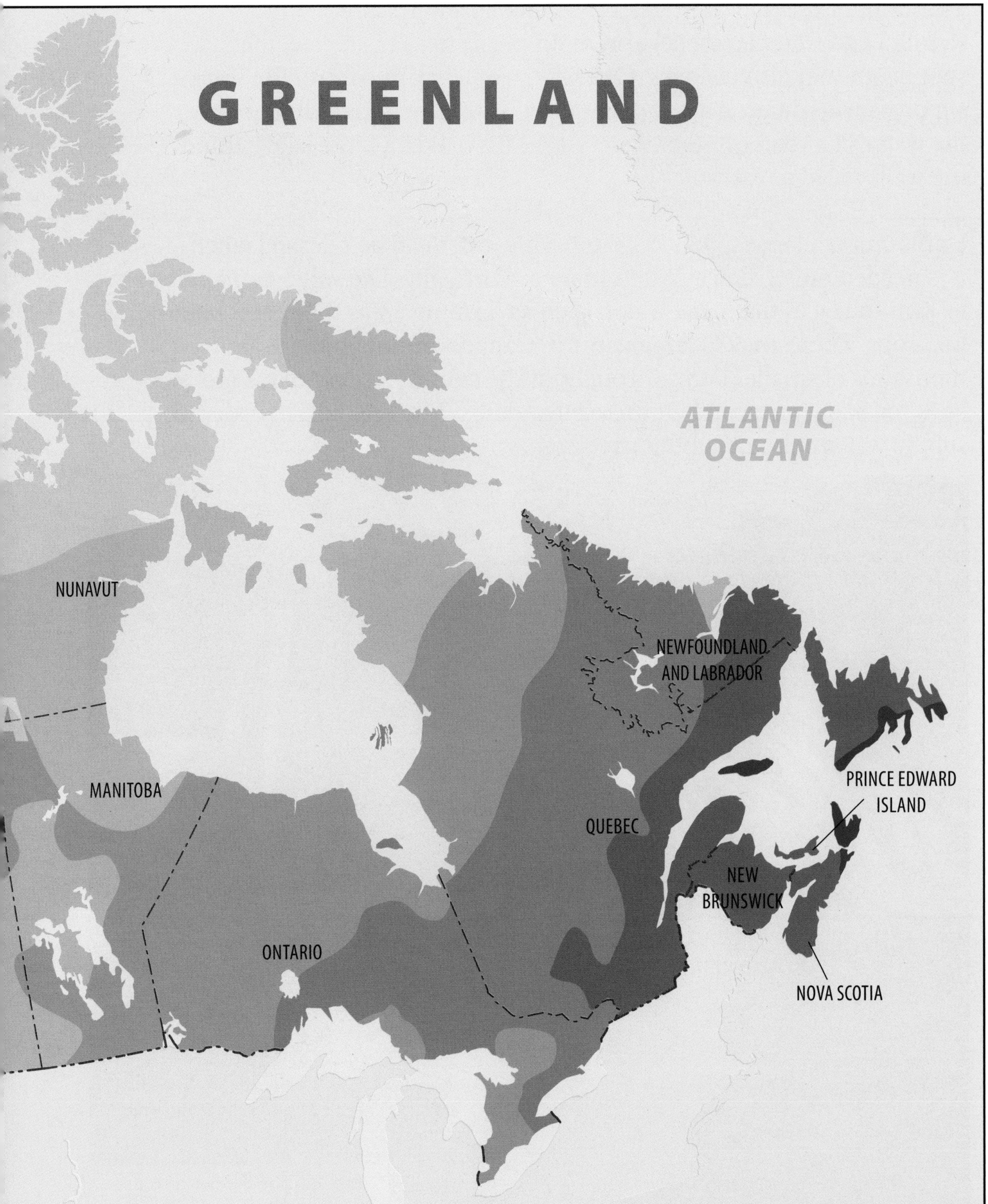

GREENLAND

*ATLANTIC
OCEAN*

NUNAVUT

NEWFOUNDLAND
AND LABRADOR

MANITOBA

PRINCE EDWARD
ISLAND

QUEBEC

NEW
BRUNSWICK

ONTARIO

NOVA SCOTIA

Dams

The amount of renewable water in Canada changes all the time. Rainfall and water levels never remain the same. This means that the supply of water also changes. One way people try to control the water supply is with dams. Dams are large walls that are built to hold back the water in a river or other waterway. This makes a large lake behind the wall, called a reservoir.

Dams create a large supply of water. This water can be released when it is needed most, such as when there is a drought. The water can also be sent to places that need water, such as farming areas that need water for crops. There are 933 large dams in Canada, although there are thousands of smaller dams throughout the country. These dams are built for many purposes. Of these large dams, 57 were built in order to supply water to homes and businesses.

Quebec has more dams than any other Canadian province.

Water Processing

Whether it comes from lakes, rivers, reservoirs, or the ground, water needs to be cleaned before it can be brought to people's homes and businesses. Water is pumped from the source and brought to a water treatment plant. At the plant, water is sent through filters, which remove any dirt and other objects. Chemicals are also added to the water to help kill germs that get through the filters. The clean water is then pumped to homes and businesses. Once it has been used, the water goes through pipes to a waste treatment plant. Here, the water is cleaned again before being returned to the river or lake.

How Canadians Get Water

Water from rivers and lakes goes through water treatment plants. Here, the water is cleaned before it is used by people. After the water is used, the dirty water enters the waste treatment plant. The water is cleaned once again before being pumped back into the lake or river.

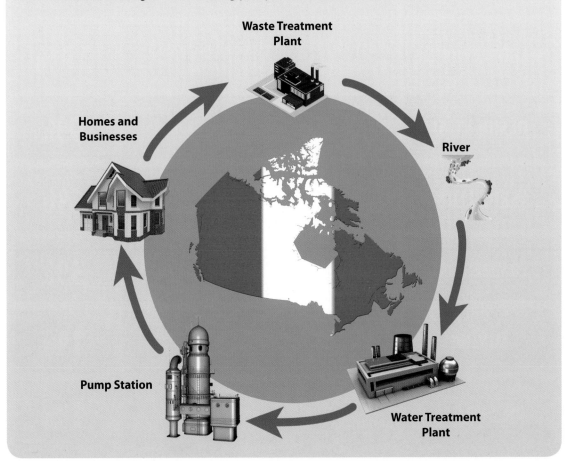

Waste Treatment Plant

Homes and Businesses

River

Pump Station

Water Treatment Plant

How Canada Uses Water

Once water has been cleaned, it can then be used by businesses and individuals. A portion of Canada's water supply is used by people in their homes. Most of the water is used by different industries and businesses, who use water as part of their everyday operations.

How Water is Used in Canada

The water used in Canada each year is divided among different areas, such as mining and manufacturing. Each area uses a certain percentage of the whole amount of water Canada uses each year.

ELECTRIC POWER	Water is used to spin turbines, which is used to make electricity.	67%
MANUFACTURING	Water may be used for heating, cooling, and as part of the products made.	13%
RESIDENTIAL	Water is used by people in their homes.	9%
AGRICULTURE	Water is used to help grow crops and as drinking water for livestock.	6%
COMMERCIAL	In stores and other businesses, water may be used for cleaning, drinking, and for other uses.	3%
MINING	Water is used to separate minerals and metals, such as gold, from rocks.	1%
OIL AND GAS	Water is used to separate oil from earth and rock.	1%

Water in the Home

Every day, people use water. They brush their teeth, wash their clothes, use the bathroom, drink, and cook with water. Each Canadian uses about 343 litres of water every day. About nine percent of Canada's total water supply is used in Canadian homes each year.

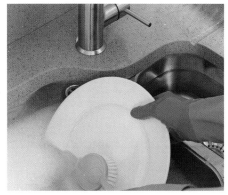

Filling the sink with soapy water rather than running water to wash dishes helps to reduce water use.

How to Use Less Water

Part of the water people use each day is used just by running the faucet. Some people let the water run while they brush their teeth, wash their hands, or when they wash the dishes. Water is also used by appliances like washing machines and dishwashers. This chart gives some suggestions on how people can lower their water use around the home.

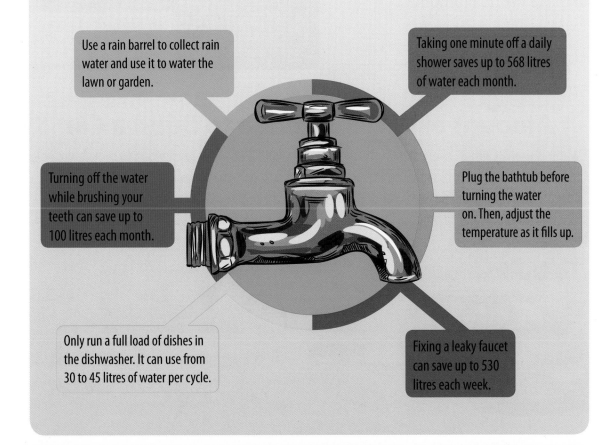

Use a rain barrel to collect rain water and use it to water the lawn or garden.

Taking one minute off a daily shower saves up to 568 litres of water each month.

Turning off the water while brushing your teeth can save up to 100 litres each month.

Plug the bathtub before turning the water on. Then, adjust the temperature as it fills up.

Only run a full load of dishes in the dishwasher. It can use from 30 to 45 litres of water per cycle.

Fixing a leaky faucet can save up to 530 litres each week.

Industry Water Use

Industry is Canada's largest water user. Industry mainly uses water for heating, cooling, and processing. Water is used to cool hot objects, such as steel that has been melted down. It is also used to cool the machines that were used to heat the steel. Heating water causes it to boil and make steam. Steam can be used to heat objects or for cleaning. Water is used during the general manufacturing process. It is used to clean machines, floors, and other surfaces in factories. It is also used to make the final product.

Industries like oil and gas use large amounts of water as part of their operations.

Amount of Water Needed to Build a Car

Water is used in almost every step of the process of making a car. Water is needed to cool down the steel and machines that are used to make the car. Each part that goes into a car also needs to be washed before it can be used. Water itself is used to make the car's tires. In total, it takes about 120,000 litres of water to produce one vehicle. This is equal to 271 bathtubs full of water.

To build a car

=

271 Bathtubs of water

Water in Food

Water is used to make food. In fact, it can take thousands of litres of water to make some foods. There are many steps in making food, and each one needs water. For example, a large amount of water goes into making a hamburger. Water is used to grow the grain the cattle eat. Every day, the cattle also need to drink water. Water is used to clean the beef when it is made into hamburger. It is also used to clean the machines that make the hamburger, which helps keep germs out of the food. Water is a part of every step along the way to making food.

Amount of Water Used to Make Food

This chart shows how much water goes into creating different kinds of food. Water is needed in almost every step of the process.

To create one piece of chocolate = **24** Bathtubs of water

To make a hamburger = **5** Bathtubs of water

To make a bag of chips = **0.4** Bathtubs of water

To grow an apple = **0.15** Bathtubs of water

Water as Electricity

Some hydroelectricity plants have been operating for more than 100 years.

Water is an important source of energy for Canada. Almost 59 percent of the electricity that Canada makes is from **hydropower**. Hydropower uses the flow of water through dams to create electricity. Hydropower dams have large turbines, which are similar to the propellers on a plane. When water flows through the dams, it spins the turbines. The spinning turbines then cause generators to spin. Generators are machines that make electricity. Canada creates more electricity than it needs. In 2009, the United States bought $2.38 billion worth of electricity from Canada.

Hydroelectricity Around the World

Electricity is measured in terawatts (TW). One terawatt is equal to 1 trillion watts. The average laptop only uses about 15 to 60 watts. Canada produces 355 terawatts of hydroelectricity per year. It is the second largest producer in the world.

LEGEND

■ Canada	■ Russia
■ United States	■ China
□ Brazil	💧 Number of Terawatts

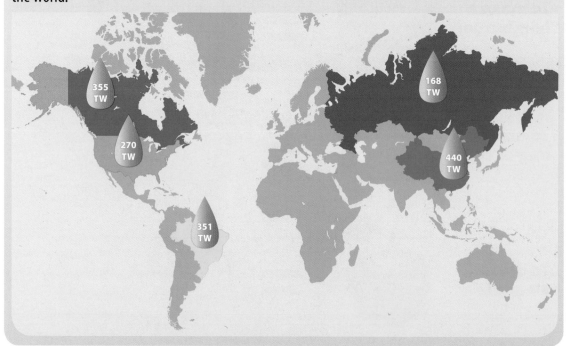

355 TW

168 TW

270 TW

440 TW

351 TW

The Water Industry

Water is an industry itself. Canada's water industry is made up of companies that help to clean water. Some of these companies make filters that help make dirty water into clean water. In Canada, the water industry is worth $7.8 billion. While significant, this is actually less than 0.01 percent of the whole economy. The water industry does important work. It helps Canadian cities and towns clean their water for their citizens.

Water samples are tested to see if water supplies contain harmful chemicals and bacteria.

Many parts of the world lack clean water. However, the Canadian government does not allow large amounts of Canada's fresh water to be sent to other countries. The government is worried that if it allowed large amounts of water to be sent to other countries, there would be no water left in Canada. Even companies that make bottled water are only allowed to use a certain amount of water each year. In Canada, there are 65 companies that bottle water. Each year they bottle about 2.3 billion litres of water. Most of this water is bottled in large containers for homes and businesses to use.

Most bottled water is used by businesses.

Water from rivers and lakes needs to be filtered before people can use it.

Water Technology

Dirty water causes sickness and death in many parts of the world. Bacteria and other germs can live in water. If a person drinks water that has germs in it, he or she can become very ill. Some diseases that people get from water can be fatal. Each year, diseases from water, such as cholera, kill about 3.4 million people around the world. Most of these people live in poor countries that cannot afford to clean their water. Though there are other ways to clean water, such as using special chemicals such as chlorine, Canadian water cleaning companies focus on UV and filtration. Chlorine was once very popular for cleaning water, but is becoming less so. This is because chlorine can have negative effects on the environment.

Filters allow water to pass through them, but stop small bits of dirt, bugs, and germs from getting through. Filters from Canadian companies are used all around the world to make water clean. Filters are sometimes used with chlorine to fully treat, or clean, the water.

As technology improves, filters are also being improved. Today, many Canadian companies are developing **microfiltration** systems. Microfiltration is similar to other kinds of filters. The difference is that new technology allows these filters to be made with very small holes. In fact, the holes are so small, even the tiniest germ cannot get through. Only water can get through. This allows water to be made clean without having to use chemicals.

Canadian companies are developing new technology for cleaning dirty water. This includes using **ultraviolet**, or UV, rays to clean water. UV light is the same light that comes from the sun. This light can kill bugs and diseases that may be in dirty water.

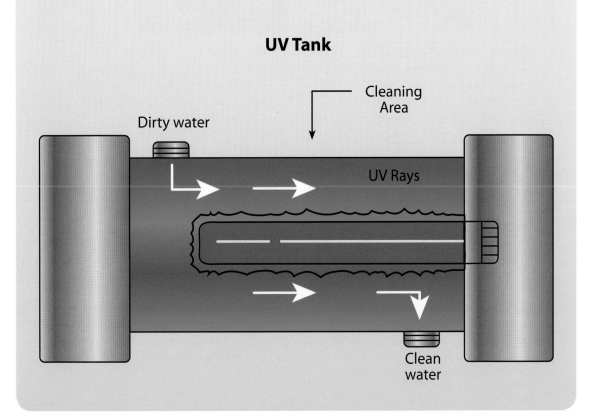

UV Cleaning Water Process

Dirty water is pumped into a tank. A UV light in the tank gives off radiation. This radiation kills all the germs in the water. Then, clean water is pumped out.

UV Tank

Dirty water

Cleaning Area

UV Rays

Clean water

Working with Water

Almost every job depends on water in some way. Some Canadians work in jobs that deal directly with water. Tens of thousands of people work in the hydropower industry. In Ontario alone, there are 3,600 jobs in this area. About 11,000 Canadians have jobs making soft drinks and ice, two products that rely on water. Fishing is another industry that relies on water. There are more than 80,000 people that work in this industry.

Water Industry Jobs

In the water industry, there are many different types of jobs. This chart shows some of the areas people work in, and some of the roles and tasks they perform.

Scientists and Environmentalists
Scientists and environmentalists do scientific research to help manage water resources and lessen the impact on the environment. They improve the quality and safety of drinking water and how water is disposed.

Engineers
Engineers plan, design, build, and analyze tools and machines for collecting, storing, cleaning, and delivering water. They research and create new processes, systems, and equipment.

Operations Workers, Maintenance Workers, and Tradespeople
Tradespeople, operations, and maintenance workers work in dams, water supply, water treatment, and waste treatment plants. They construct and maintain water treatment systems.

Policy and Planning Advisors
Policy and planning advisors give advice to companies and governments on what rules should be put in place to help manage water use.

Water Jobs

There is a wide range of jobs within the water industry. Each job has different tasks to perform and requires a certain type of training.

Hydrologist

Duties: Study water and the environment
Education: University degree in science or engineering

Hydrologists study how water affects people and how people affect water. They study how new buildings may affect nearby water supplies. Some hydrologists try to show farmers better ways to use the water to help them grow more crops.

Plumber

Duties: Build and fix water systems in buildings
Education: College certification and on-the-job training

Plumbers make sure the water supply is safe and clean for houses and businesses. They build the systems that move clean water to where it can be used. They also build the systems that move used, dirty water to sewers and water treatment plants.

Fishers

Duties: Catch fish and other marine animals
Education: On-the-job training

Fishers catch marine animals, such as fish, lobsters, and crabs, for food. They often work for themselves and sell their catch to other companies. Working on the ocean can be dangerous. Fishers often work on a boat that is far from land. They must be ready for poor weather and water conditions.

Managing Water

Water is used by every living organism. In Canada, water supports thousands of species of animals. It helps forests grow, and gives many living things, such as fish, a place to live.

Governments

Governments set rules that guide how water can be used. These rules state the amount of water that can be used each day. They also tell what must be done to clean any dirty water before it is sent back into rivers and lakes. Some bodies of water are protected by the government from industrial use.

Individuals

Individuals have an effect on the amount of water they use in their homes. People collect water from showers or washing machines. This water, called greywater, is used to water lawns. Some people buy water efficient appliances that use less water. They also may report any pollution they find in water sources to the government.

Since water is such an important resource, people, governments, and companies must be very careful about how they use it. These individuals and groups work together to make sure that Canada's water resources are used properly. They also make sure the environment is affected as little as possible.

Companies

Companies hire environmental experts to learn about better ways to use water. They sometimes invest millions of dollars to find ways to use less water. Companies also look for new water-saving technologies. For example, some oil companies are developing ways to use salt water instead of fresh water to get oil. This would leave more fresh water for people.

Environmental Groups

Environmental groups work with governments and companies to make sure that companies are following the rules and using water correctly. These groups are also involved in protecting important water sources. The work of environmental groups can help protect Canada's water resources.

Quiz

What country is ahead of Canada in the production of hydropower?

China

How many companies bottle water in Canada?

65

What percentage of Canada's electricity is produced by hydropower?

59 percent

How much water does the average Canadian use each day?

About 343 litres

What percentage of the world is covered in water?

About 70 percent

What percentage of the world's renewable water supply is in Canada?

About 9 percent

What percentage of Earth's water is fresh water?

About 2.5 percent

What percentage of Canadians get their water from groundwater sources?

About 25 percent

Further Resources

Websites to check out!

Kids Zone
www.enwin.com/kids/water/

Environment Canada
www.ec.gc.ca/eau-water

Water Conservation
www.naturecanada.ca/water_facts.html

Activity

Make your own water filter

Materials Needed: 2-litre soda bottle cut in half (have an adult cut the bottle), paper towels, gravel, small pebbles, sand, cotton balls, dirty water (make your own by adding cooking oil, dirt, food colouring, or pieces of paper).

Water is often dirty and needs to be cleaned before it can be used. In this activity, you will make your own water filter.

1. Turn the top half of the bottle upside-down and place it inside the bottom half. The top of the bottle will be where the filter goes. The bottom half will hold the filtered water.
2. Place a folded paper towel in the top half of the bottle. Layer the gravel, small pebbles, sand, and cotton balls on top of the paper towel. Put the sand in first, then the small pebbles, gravel, and cotton balls.
3. Pour the dirty water through the filter. Record your findings. Is the filtered water clean? Experiment with different ways of layering the filter. Try different filter materials, such as a sponge or cloth.

Key Words

hydropower: energy that is created by the flow of water

microfiltration: a type of filtration that removes objects from fluids

non-renewable: a resource that cannot be replaced once it is used

precipitation: water in the form of rain or snow that falls to the ground

renewable: a resource that can be replaced once it is used

ultraviolet: a type of radiation invisible to the human eye

Index